Getting St

FREE RESOURCES

Over 14,000 people receive my regular, free emails
with stories, games and teaching techniques
that support the ideas in this book.

Sign up or enquire about training and
workshops for your school at:

www.thephilosophyman.com

one
slice
books

Published by:

The Philosophy Man Ltd
7 Tower Road, Writtle
Chelmsford, CM1 3NR, UK

Email: jason@thephilosophyman.com
Web: www.thephilosophyman.com
Tel: +44 (0) 1245 830123

All rights reserved. No part of this publication may be reproduced, stored in a retrieval system or transmitted in any form, or by any means, electronic, mechanical, photocopying, recording or otherwise, without the prior permission of the publishers.

Design by Kerim Hudson
© Jason Buckley 2011

Contents

Stages of Enquiry

Introduction

"Sir, can't you just give us the answer?"

I remember this response from a pupil bored of three or four failed attempts to guess an answer which he knew I knew already. This sort of classroom dialogue is rather like a drawn-out game of snap. While necessary for checking understanding, it's not real, responsive dialogue at all. Everything said could come from the teacher, who as well as knowing the answer chooses the questions and decides who answers. Pupils join in, but as volunteers from the audience in the teacher's show.

In philosophy for children (P4C), rather than being that "sage on the stage", teachers facilitate as "a guide on the side". Learners form a community of enquiry, arranged in a circle so that they (literally) look to one another for answers instead of to the teacher. In response to thought provoking stimuli, they create and select their own questions - ones to which sir can't just give the answer because sir, like everyone else, is still puzzling it out.

In the pages that follow, you'll find a description of one particular P4C enquiry, and alternatives for the various stages of a common method of doing P4C. These pages are marked out with coloured page edges. Even experienced practitioners should find some new ideas, and a handy source of reminders.

There are also some tips on the subtle craft of facilitation, sections on fitting P4C into a crowded curriculum, the benefits of doing so, and some pages suggesting further resources.

This guide inevitably focuses on surface procedures, which are easier to convey in brief than the values that stand behind them. However, P4C is about more than a particular structure, just as it is about more than getting children talking (if that's all you want to do, release a snake in assembly - they'll be talking about it for months). I've attempted to articulate some of the values I see in P4Cing in "The Spirit of Enquiry". These values have strong appeal for adults as well, and although I use "pupils" for brevity most of the guide applies equally to philosophy in communities.

A few thank yous. P4C emerged from the work of Matthew Lipman, a US philosophy professor. He wanted his undergraduates to think for themselves, not just to ingest answers they could regurgitate in exams. Both he and his collaborator Ann Sharp died in 2010, leaving a diverse P4C community that is active in over sixty countries. Given the inordinate amount of time I have taken to rewrite this tiny book!, I am boggled by their prolific, decades-long body of work.

The UK has its own vibrant P4C community, led by SAPERE (see p34). I have picked up many of the ideas in this book from SAPERE trainers and other colleagues. It would be intolerably stop-start if I mentioned every source of every idea (and it's not easy to trace the source of many), so instead I've credited as many as I can at www.thephilosophyman.com/thanks

Thanks also to my graphic designer, Kerim Hudson, for helping me squeeze as much into these pages as possible. Most importantly, thanks to you on behalf of your enquirers for looking into P4C and giving it a go. If you have any questions (or answers) about P4C, my email and mobile are at the end.

One Example of an Enquiry

To get the most from this minibook, receive sustained support from the free, weekly Pocket P4C email bulletin. The resources for this enquiry are in Issue 1. Register on the homepage of:

www.thephilosophyman.com

P4Cers prefer the term "enquiry" to "lesson". It signals an active, shared pursuit of the truth, not a time to soak up knowledge from the teacher. This particular enquiry raises themes of fairness and equality, but not all enquiries involve ethics. Each of the stages outlined here could also be done in many different ways.

Everyone is sat in a circle. To help with getting set, the facilitator lays out four cards with ways an imaginary teacher might be unfair - such as treating you better because she likes you, or because you are like her. Pupils stand by the one they think is worst and a few then give their "best reason" for choosing it.

The class now hears the stimulus - today, the story of an imaginary teacher who treats all his students the same - giving them identical praise, detentions and grades.

Next, pupils have some private thinking time to respond to the stimulus and choose three words that are important to the story. Then they form five small groups and share their ideas.

This leads on to question making as each group writes a juicy, philosophical question on a sheet of paper in marker pen.

Then comes question airing. Pupils read their questions twice over, before laying them in the centre of the circle. Volunteers rearrange them to show links they see between the questions.

After that question choosing, this time an invisible vote. They face out, hands behind backs, giving a thumbs up to those they find interesting. "Is there such a thing as fairness?" is chosen.

In first thoughts, the pupils who framed the question explain their thinking. The facilitator asks anyone who disagrees with them to comment next, establishing a starting range of opinions.

The building stage is the heart of the enquiry. Each speaker gives a thumbs up signal to pass the discussion to the next person waiting to speak. It goes back and forth across the circle, and they are sticklers for giving everyone a fair turn. They agree and disagree with each other, giving reasons and examples.

The facilitator intervenes at times, to probe deeper, or help them make connections. He lets a digression run into why "fairness" would be a word if there were no such thing. Then he recalls them to their main trail - whether everything must be unfair to someone, or whether real fairness can be achieved if you try.

In last thoughts, everyone has a final opportunity to speak. For some, the question has been settled. For others, there are more questions than ever. Later, in a review of the session, the participants will think about the process rather than the particular question: how had they grown as a community of enquiry from their last session, and how they want to grow in the future.

Getting Set

First, sort out the space: insist on a neat circle, or if you can't clear away the furniture, set up a "parliament" with you in the speaker's chair and the back rows sitting on tables. Recap the rules (not too many - it kills it): give everyone a turn, disagree without being disagreeable, speak to the enquiry not the facilitator.

Sometimes (post-PE?), you might need an "inactivity" to calm them down such as restful music or a breathing exercise. In general, though, warm-up games that involve some physical or intellectual energy and playfulness help to "sell" P4C from the start. At a deeper level, philosophy, like play, involves a certain freedom of spirit, and a willingness to get involved, take risks and take a turn as the centre of attention. A game signals a shift to this mindset which then persists into the main enquiry.

Teamwork games

These games improve pupils' awareness of each other so that they notice when others want to speak.

All sit down – the group have to sit down one at a time without talking to each other. If two sit down at once, all have to stand up again. It can also be done by counting up from one to the number in the class.

Shrinking Mexican wave – make a movement which is copied in a wave around the circle. Start with large movements and finish with tiny ones that require careful attention.

Thinkers' Games – many successful warm-up games, including the three below, share this underlying structure:

Think about a question with competing reasonable answers.
Commit to an answer publicly (move yourself/something).
Justify your decision with your best reasons.
Reflect on what's been said and show if it's changed your mind.

Everyone's thinking can be seen, so pupils are curious to hear why others thought as they did. "Why did you think that?" draws a shy child in more gently than "What do you think?"; and more of the talk takes place standing, mimicking children's social talk - so you get broader participation. Some examples are given below, or see "Thinkers Games", the second book in this series.

Vote with your feet – possible answers to a question such as, "Which of these would you rather be?" are placed on separate sheets around the circle. Pupils stand by their choice. After hearing others' reasons, some may move, which is very affirming for the person who gave the reason.

Philosopher's fruit salad – "Swap places across the circle...
    ...if you think you can ever have everything you need."
    ...if you think you can ever have everything you want."
    ...if you think you need *not* to have everything you want."

Conceptometer – e.g. each group has a set of A4 sheets with scenarios, and must arrange them into an "Evilometer" from good to evil. Or do it as a **Sort Yourselves Out** activity where each player holds a card and they all form a line.

Presentation (Stimulus)

The stimulus provides a shared starting point for your enquiry. Its obvious role within this sequence is to raise themes and provoke the creation of interesting questions. A good stimulus, though, will often be sticky - compelling enough to provide a shared context that speakers return to during the discussion - "It's like in the story when..."

Let what you choose speak for itself. If you give an interpretation, pupils will follow your lead. Once used to framing philosophical questions, an enquiry can be set off by almost anything. The easiest stimuli to begin with are first on this list.

- *Picture books* – best projected somehow for large groups.
- *Story* – read or told. Fables, fairy tales, parables.
- *Dialogues* – read out by pupils.
- *Reportage* – historical recounts, narrations of discoveries.
- *Extracts from studied texts* – e.g. last page of a book.
- *Combined warm-up/stimulus* – e.g. a "Conceptometer".
- *News story* – in print or video.
- *Video clip* – an advert, film or TV extract.
- *Photos* – perhaps taken by the pupils to show a concept.
- *Work of art* – e.g. Guernica, Holbein Henry VIII.
- *Music* – a song or for a real challenge, instrumental.
- *Object* – a flag, a historical artefact, a product.
- *Happening* – school trip, practical challenge, a visit.

You can also juxtapose two stimuli to highlight a contrast.

A successful stimulus is likely to exhibit at least two of these:

Concepts – it raises a big idea like love, opposites like rich and poor, or neighbouring concepts like pretending and lying.

Tension – it pulls in two directions at once. If you see a picture of Belsen, you know what to think; if you see a soldier wearing a swastika smiling at an admiring child, you have more work to do.

Humanity – even if it's about animals! Characters to empathise with give a problem urgency, and make a stimulus more "sticky".

Argument – the original materials for P4C by Lipman and Sharp featured children pondering and arguing about interesting ideas, providing a model for dialogue.

Aesthetic appeal – things that are worth reading/seeing in their own right, not just to "function" as a stimulus.

Other options to bear in mind:

- *Familiarity* – if pupils know a topic, a small reminder of it may be charged with meaning e.g. a poppy.
- *Shock value* – to energise a new group.
- *Topical examples* – can give urgency to eternal questions.
- *Breadth* – different aspects inviting a range of questions.
- *Narrowness* – something that steers thinking towards a topic you need to cover.
- *The interests of the group* – a practised group may take responsibility for their own stimuli.

Thinking Time

Before coming up with possible questions for the enquiry, it's good to have some thinking time individually or in groups. In the case of a story, this is partly to secure an understanding of what happened. While you silently re-present the stimulus, or they re-read it, you might offer some prompts for quiet, individual thinking, such as:

> What are your feelings about it?
> What interested you?
> What confused you?
> Put yourself in the shoes of...
> What provoked a reaction from you?
> What questions do you have about it?

Or suggest an outcome to focus their reflections, such as:

> List three key ideas.
> Draw a mind map.
> Represent your ideas in a picture or cartoon.
> Retell the story in ten words or less.
> Write your thoughts in a brief paragraph.

The activity I use most often is a concept pool. Give groups a few minutes to find five ideas/words/phrases/opinions they think are important in the story. Ideally, write each word on a separate sheet of scrap paper so that they can be pooled together in the middle of the circle, or record them onto a whiteboard or flipchart. This creates a shared resource for formulating questions and enriching the discussion.

Taboo – describe what the story is about without mentioning any of the characters or events! Forces thinking on to the concepts that underpin the story.

Thought gallery – write or draw thoughts on signed post-its or slips of paper which can be displayed on chairs or walls. Pupils walk round, browsing each others' thoughts.

Z to A – within small groups, in first name order starting at Z and going back to A, each person voices their ideas. Good for new groups as it doubles as an introduction.

Cocktail party – pair, share, change partners, share again.

Classroom activities tend to work from the individual out towards the group - for example, Think-Pair-Share. That has the advantage that people can decide what they think before they are overwhelmed by someone else's ideas. However, people often have more to think about after they have spoken to others. So a brief bit of group talk before some private thinking can help people get started. Just telling children to sit quietly and "think about the stimulus" won't get you far, certainly in the early stages.

That "Share-Think" pattern fits with one of the ideals of P4C - that the habits of thinking that start out as distributed around the group become internalised as part of the thinking repertoire of the individual. After a while of enquiring together, I can carry inside my head the skills of Alex who always come up with examples from Dr Who, Roxana who likes to get inside the mind of the character in the story, Alice who creates similes such as "happiness is like a cake, and you need..."

Question Making

"Are dreams real?"
"Can you change your fate?"
"Can animals speak?"

"Who made God?"
"What is a true friend?"
"Is lying sometimes good?"

All these are juicy, philosophical questions that can lead to rich discussions, with differing opinions that can be supported by reasons and examples. A key democratic feature of P4C is that questions should come from the pupils, not the teacher.

It's a skill that develops with practice. Usually, getting each group of four or five to create one question is best. Prime them with examples of juicy questions during warm-up games, and be prepared to help them formulate their ideas into questions.

Early questions can be very rooted in the text, but you need ones that must be answered by discussion, not comprehension. To break that habit, you can ask for everybody questions that would make sense to someone who hadn't heard the story.

Sometimes you can turn a question that seems very textual into an expanding question. "Did Macbeth see a dagger?" invites discussion of how reliable our senses are in telling us about the world. "Why was the gruffalo scared of the mouse?" leads to discussing where fears come from, and if fear is a good thing.

Another way of following the children's interests is to start with a question of your own, but be alert for an emerging question to come from the group once the discussion is underway.

You may find the following question quadrant, a variation on Phil Cam's, useful for your own thinking or to share with children.

Different disciplines serve questions to different parts of the quadrant. If the answer is in the text for all to see and agree, it might be suitable for comprehension in English. If the question requires us to imagine something new in the world of the story, it suits a creative response. Questions concerning our world, but that you could ask an expert and receive an answer to which all could agree, are good for research, science, perhaps history.

It's the questions which both concern our world and on which reasonable people can argue the merits of different answers that are best for enquiry.

about the characters or story
"What did Jack do with his fortune?"
"Where did Jack get the beans?"
Stimulus/story world

Look in the text
Imagine a possibility

Agree
one accepted answer

Argue
competing reasonable answers

Ask an expert
Enquiry together

"Who is the world's tallest giant?"
Our world
provoked by the story but going beyond it
"Does being rich make you happy?"

12

"It's not a silly question if you can't answer it." Jostein Gaarder

Getting each group to write its question on a separate sheet of paper or mini-whiteboard gives you flexibility. Or they can be written onto a flipchart or whiteboard. Some people swear by the principle of getting them to write their names next to the question to increase their sense of ownership; for me, it takes too long and makes choosing the question unnecessarily personalised.

Suitable questions...	**Unsuitable questions...**
...will divide opinion.	...may be googlable/factual. Writing a factual question on one side of a sheet and a philosophical question on the other shows this distinction.
...contain big ideas.	
...are provoked by the stimulus, not random whims. "What's the meaning of life," while interesting, only has a shared context for the whole community if the question is relevant to what they saw.	...may be about the stimulus, not its themes. Such questions can often be made juicier by generalising them.
...may use why, should.	...may be speculative. "What happened next?", "Will we ever land on Mars?"
...may be a search for meanings or definitions.	
...can be closed (yes/no answers) if the reasons why are open to argument.	...may be questions of taste which are hard to argue.

Question Airing

Reflecting about the questions chosen can inform the voting, raise issues that will feature in the subsequent discussion, and develop an awareness of what makes a good question for future enquiries. Sometimes, though, you might prefer to go straight to the vote to conserve time for the main discussion.

Question quadrant – use the quadrant two pages back to work out which questions can be answered in other ways.

Snap/Connections – with questions on individual sheets, a volunteer arranges them to show any that can be "merged" for voting, and to reflect connections between others; a second volunteer rearranges them to show different connections.

Explaining – question creators explain why they thought the question would be interesting.

Celebrating – pupils say why they think a question someone else has asked will be interesting.

One minute wonder – discuss each for one minute.

Question Oscars – nominate hardest/easiest to answer, most controversial, most important.

Question the question – what further questions will each question lead to? Helps with the quality of future questions.

Question Choosing

This is an important stage, because the whole community of enquiry comes together to take ownership of the rest of the enquiry. People have more to say about questions that interest them, and those whose questions aren't chosen can see it's fair.

Emphasise that the vote is for a juicy question that will make for an interesting and sustained discussion. I usually allow votes for your own question, and find that votes are cast on merit, not friendship. A good thing to point out the first time you vote is that at an election, once the polls open, campaigning stops. It's a good rule to enforce to avoid excitable canvassing.

Note the runner-up in case the first one dies a death. Sometimes people vote for a question they have a strong opinion on, only for it to turn out to be the same strong opinion as everyone else.

How many votes?

Simple vote – vote once only.

Multivote – you have, say, three votes and can share them between questions (e.g. one hand up, two hands up, or stand up to cast all three at once).

Omnivote – vote for as many as you like.

Analogue democracy – use applause which offers a continuum from polite ripple to rapturous cheers.

Ways of voting

Voting with your feet – if the questions are on big sheets of paper, you can lay them on the floor and ask pupils to stand by the one they want, or to make a "human bar chart" by forming lines starting at each question.

Question gallery – if there are lots of questions, I skip the airing stage, place questions on chairs, and give each pupil three chopped down post-its to distribute as votes.

Read them out – one after the other, counting and recording votes as you go. Secret voting avoids a popularity contest and also focuses minds on the questions heard. Open voting can be faster and seems more grown-up. Different signals can be used.

Open voting	Secret voting
Hands up	*Blind* – heads down, eyes shut, hands up.
Thumbs up	
	Invisible – all stand, face out, hands behind backs, thumbs up to vote yes.
Stand up	
Step forward	

Not voting at all

What if someone's questions never get chosen? Or boys vote as a block? Or they want you to choose for them? Or a subject is always avoided? Could you have a vote not to have a vote?

First Thoughts

The important thing is that everybody gets to talk to somebody before anybody has to speak to everybody. It's hard to listen until *someone* has heard the point you are itching to make. In pairs or groups, think of possible answers, examples or ways to tackle the question, then kick off the whole group enquiry with:

Warm-up lap – in a small group you can hear from everybody (or allow them to "pass") but it's "creeping death" if there are 30.

Big thumb/little thumb – partners go thumb to thumb and either big or little thumbians report back.

Hot potato – groups that have been sharing ideas stack fists (potatoes). Then ask, e.g. "third potato down" to report back.

Questioner introduces – the simplest beginning is for one of those who asked the question to explain their view (if they haven't at the airing stage).

Opinion compass – get a pupil who has a strong opinion about the question to speak first, then invite a comment from someone who disagrees with their point. Next take two other opposed points that take a different approach to the question.

Dividing line – if the question can have a yes or no answer, pupils position themselves either side of a line to show their position on the question, with their best reasons at the ready.

Building

This is the core of the enquiry, and the stage where the teacher's role is most different to regular classwork. A very important move in shifting the focus from you to them is handing over traffic control. Encourage priority for those who have spoken less, and point out people who have been waiting if necessary, but as much as possible, let each speaker choose the next.

It's only when that happens that they begin to look and speak to each other rather than to you, and to sustain rallies of contributions amongst themselves rather than waiting for you to echo, validate or discard each utterance. Children are so used to looking at you, let them know it's not rude to not!

The phrase, "a pass it on discussion" is useful, and can be used in regular lessons as well. Choose the signals you will use.

One signal – hands up is simple and helps shyer members get noticed. A thumb up is less tiring and can double as a positive signal to the next speaker.

Two signals – thumb up to follow on, hand up for a new trail.

Ace – an extra signal, to be used once only by each pupil when he has an urgent point e.g. standing up.

No signal – just watch each other and talk naturally, giving way if two start at once. Takes maturity and consideration.

"Are they thinking? Are they thinking for themselves?"
Roger Sutcliffe

Relinquishing traffic control doesn't mean you sit back with nothing to do! If you just let things take their own sweet way, it can easily degenerate into undemanding swapping of anecdotes, or grind to a halt. When they stop talking, or carry on talking but stop thinking, or go off at a tangent that is unhelpful, you must judge how to intervene to reinvigorate, deepen or refocus the discussion. But intervene too often, and it's just your lesson, not everyone's enquiry.

Something that is very helpful is to create some "questions in waiting" while they are getting their first thoughts together. These are connected questions you might use to prompt fresh thinking during this specific enquiry. There are also general techniques you can use. I use physical terms for ease of recall.

UP/DOWN: In this detail of Rafael's "School of Athens", Plato points up to the heavens, to ideas in their pure forms, while Aristotle signals a more "down to earth" approach. If an enquiry becomes a story-swapping session, go up a level and ask for links between them. If it loses focus, ground it by asking for examples.

If the discussion stalls, or to engage more speakers, FASTER:

Back into groups/pairs – a good strategy for half-time.

Cat among the pigeons – if the group are being shy and sluggish, acting dumb and posing a mildly outrageous question will usually liven them up.

Get physical – get people to stand to show their opinion about an issue that has emerged. Lets you gently bring in people who have not spoken. "Donna, why did you think...?"

Question time –when a new question arises, ask a panel of three or four pupils to give their views. Start just before someone who hasn't spoken to draw him in but give him time to think.

If talking outpaces listening or points don't connect, SLOWER:

Famous last words – praise the contribution of a dominant speaker, then promise him the final say in Last Thoughts, which he can prepare as he listens. Or have three "lives" for comments.

Chain of ten – the next ten speakers must agree or disagree with the previous speaker in the chain.

Conch – an object that must be passed/thrown from speaker to speaker. Gives prestige to the speaker and helps sustain a good "rally". Don't use a ball as not everyone thinks he can catch. A brightly coloured silk scarf, knotted at one end with a tail that unfurls in mid-air, is the deluxe option.

Last Thoughts

Towards the end of the enquiry, it can be good to focus in on a few answers that have emerged, testing them against examples and evidence. You will rarely reach a consensus, but it allows people to make a judgement about where they stand and provides a sense of progress.

Whether you have got close to some specific answers or not, try to leave time to finish rather than stop. As at the beginning, always give people a chance to talk in pairs or groups first. Most of the structures in first thoughts can be repeated here to "bookend" the enquiry. Some other options:

Three words only or only questions allowed

Get physical – stand to indicate the answer you most agree with, or to show you think something else.

Changed minds – swap places if you have changed your mind about something.

Say thanks – stand next to someone who said something you found interesting. You'll need to shout "freeze" as some people should be chasing one another.

Listeners' time – hear from those who have only spoken once or not at all. Some P4Cers always allow a child to "pass". I prefer a strong presumption that everyone will speak at some point, as children who don't want to speak may "want to want" to do so.

Review

Taking time to reflect on how a session went is important. It helps a community to build on strengths and address weaknesses; it extends the democratic element from choosing questions to planning enquiries; it shows you are getting somewhere.

Perhaps most importantly, it is a time to think about the thinking that took place. Such moments happen throughout the enquiry process, but it is important to make that "metacognition" explicit.

Question Questions – what made it an interesting question? Did we stick to it? Should we have done? Why did people vote for it? What can we learn for the next time we write questions?

PMQ – pluses, minuses, questions is a standard tool.

Philosophy bingo – use the card on p27 to identify habits that were or were not shown during an enquiry.

Match highlights – what were some of the specific moves people made that helped the enquiry?

Growth points – how had we improved from the previous enquiry? How would we like to improve in the next one?

O.W. – how can we follow through in the "outside world" beyond the enquiry? Research, testing what we thought in practice, or taking action?

Philosophical Moves

The more subtle aspect of the facilitator's job is not the mechanics of keeping a discussion going, but the art of probing for depth and encouraging pupils to challenge their own thinking and that of others.

As well as thinking about big concepts such as fairness, love, beauty, you want pupils to become fluent in the little concepts you think *with*, such as similarity, evidence, examples.

One way to do this is to encourage philosophical "moves" within the enquiry. There are three main ways to do this: requesting a particular move, acknowledging when a pupil has already used one, or pushing the current speaker to think more deeply with direct probing. Don't overdo the last one, or it can revert to you directing everything, and beware of echoing every contribution. You can often bring in an appropriate label for the move at the same time. Here are some common moves.

Reasoning – So your reason supports Jack's point?

Examples – Could someone give us an example of courage?

Defining – What do you mean by...? Give us a definition.

Finding evidence – What would support that view?

Implications – If you think ... does that mean ...

Spotting connections – Does that connect with Tia's point?

Contradiction – Can Fred and Jenny both be right? Or do they contradict each other?

Clarification – Now Ali has been really precise about what he means, does anyone agree or disagree?

Uncertainty – You think we can't be sure because...

Consequences – What would that mean for...

Consistency – Can you ... if you believe that...?

Principles – What's the big idea behind that?

Generalising – So is that always true?

Particularising – How would that apply to this school?

Distinctions – Is the case John describes different?

Lastly, because most importantly, justifying. Everyday "reasonableness" often stops at "everyone's entitled to their own opinion". That is just a precondition of enquiry, not its object. Giving reasons for opinions is the start. Asking a "second why" to find out why a reason is important begins to open up the key inisight that some reasons are better than others.

4 Cs Thinking

Community of enquiry is a balance. If all you want is good participation and listening, you will have a pleasant community but not much enquiry. If a few dominate or you intervene constantly, you may have a rigorous enquiry but it won't belong to the community.

These "4Cs" are reminders of this balance, together with quick suggestions for boosting each element.

community

Caring thinking – not just interpersonal caring (encourage the use of names in passing on) but taking a deep interest in questions that matter. Use stimuli with an emotional impact.

Collaborative thinking – listening so that ideas are built together. Encourage pupils to say how their point connects with the previous speaker.

enquiry

Creative thinking – using imagination, alternatives, analogies. Introduce metaphors – "If happiness were a cake, what would it be made of?

Critical thinking – testing for truth, clarifying meanings. Once some possible answers to the question have been identified, shift into "evidence mode" – what supports each answer?

A breakdown of the 4Cs into more specific skills can be seen in the bingo card opposite.

Collaborative	Caring	Creative	Critical	
Most people participating	Reflecting about the stimulus	Thinking "what if..?"	Finding the big ideas	Giving evidence
Building on each other's ideas	Respecting each speaker	Thinking "so then..?"	Picking out the little details	Questioning assumptions and evidence
Disagreeing without being disagreeable	Taking an interest in other views	Seeing connections	Defining meanings	Finding criteria
Encouraging atmosphere	Open to changing ideas	Finding examples	Drawing distinctions	Judging reasons

3 Cs Concepts

4 Cs thinking gives an idea of the "how" of P4C. The "what" may be understood by seeing P4C as a conceptual education. The richest enquiries tend to involve concepts which are:

Common – shared by everybody, and not just the preserve of some group of specialists.

Central – important to us in how we live our lives and understand the world and each other.

Contestable – the subject of argument and competing understandings.

Concepts are often best explored in pairs with their opposites or neighbours. Over time you might choose stimuli that give the opportunity to explore some of these concepts and others.

fairness, equality	language, meaning
reality, illusion	goodness, politeness
work, play	permanence, change
morality, law	science, arts, humanities
happiness	beauty, ugliness
belief, knowledge	needs, wants
friendship, independence	wealth, poverty
progress, tradition	truth, deceit, pretending
freedom, compulsion	causation, coincidence
celebrity, talent, merit	proof, prejudice
youth, age	justice, injustice

Concept Stretchers

This is Roger Sutcliffe's useful name for exercises and discussion plans to encourage detailed thinking about specific concepts. These were integral to the original P4C materials, and without them, it takes very skilful facilitation to make P4C an education in thinking rather than just a ritualised conversation.

Conceptometers are one form of concept stretcher (pg6). Another method is to take a pair of neighbouring or opposite concepts, and brainstorm questions about them, perhaps arranging them with the harder questions at the end.

Are all celebrities talented?
Are all talented people celebrities?
Can you be born a celebrity? Can you make yourself a celebrity?
Can you be born talented? Can you make yourself talented?
Is being a celebrity a talent of its own?
Would you rather be an untalented celebrity or an uncelebrated talent?

Or you could use examples. Which of these is a talent?

Playing the piano
Saying a tongue-twister
Teaching a good lesson
Working hard

Playing the fool
Making a million pounds
Getting full marks in a test
Becoming talented

A deeper exploration of concept stretchers is available to subscribers of www.p4c.com; or google "Philosophical discussion plans and exercises" for an article by Lipman.

P4C in the Curriculum

In a humane education, children of all ages should have an hour a week set aside for P4C or something very like it, in which they can identify and develop their interests in their own questions, not someone else's. English, Citizenship, RE and PSHE are also obvious homes – but P4C can enrich any subject.

Bookending – using P4C enquiries to start and finish units of work, establishing the themes and then returning to them with greater sophistication.

The big picture – why is your subject important? What values or habits of mind do you need to have to be a good scientist? What are the big ethical issues?

Topicality – use a subject-related news story as a stimulus to establish the relevance of your subject.

Exam practice – prepare for extended writing tasks with an enquiry chosen from past exam questions.

Question criteria – finding space for an enquiry in your scheme of work may sometimes require that the discussion covers a specific topic. Set that as a criterion for acceptable questions. Don't feel guilty about not being a "P4C purist"!

Philosophic topic – plan from the topic to the big concepts it touches on, through questions about those concepts, to activities and stimuli within the topic that raise those questions.

Writing and P4C

For some pupils, one of the attractions of P4C as usually practised is that it does not involve writing. At the risk of squandering this selling point, here are some suggestions for writing within P4C.

Dialogues – write a dialogue in play script or direct speech form, about the question chosen (or the one you wanted). Good for building self-esteem and stamina as a writer.

Written last words – individual written responses are pinned on the wall around the question.

Thinkbook – an exercise book with a different question as the title on each page, and space for the writers' own. Responses can be in dialogue form or continuous prose.

Philosophy journal – a small, diary sized notebook (of the size often used for spellings) to record personal reflections after each enquiry.

Match report – a back-pages style report on the enquiry. Persuasive or discursive writing that emerges from P4C may show improved structure and expression because its content is already developed.

Home-school dialogues – get children and parents to talk about philosophical questions at home and record what each thinks. (See Sara Stanley's *"But Why?"*)

Juicy Questions

"Juicy" is a catchy name for enquiry questions. Some of these echo debates in philosophy as studied in universities. Others are more playful and have been road-tested with a wide range of ages. Pick one for a mini-enquiry when the opportunity arises.

Is luck real?
What is happiness?
What is a true friend?
Is this a real question?
Can you think wordlessly?
What is a fair punishment?
Can you escape your fate?
What does it mean to be free?
Would living forever be boring?
Is it possible to predict the future?
Rich and ugly, or poor and pretty?
Is it fair to treat everybody the same?
Is it always good to pursue your dream?
Is it fair to expect the rich to pay for the poor?
Would 2+2 still be 4 if there was no-one to count?
Is it better to be a happy pig or an unhappy professor?
When people thought slavery was right, were they wrong?
Are you the same person you were a year ago?
Is there anything you can know for certain?
How do you know if anyone else is real?
Is the hole in a donut part of the donut?
Are some rules meant to be broken?
Can it ever be wrong to forgive?

Scary Questions

Children will sometimes choose a question that makes you or a child in the group feel uncomfortable and exposed. You may also actively choose a stimulus that you think will raise a topic that is "taboo" but important, such as race, religion, sexuality, or death.

People often overestimate what should be tackled as it arises, and underestimate what can be tackled with some sensitive planning. Not every question is "P4Cable" not all enquiries have to be tackled in single sessions. You might adjourn the enquiry to give you time to think, and consider using the strategies below.

Remember that you're still the teacher. You don't enter a mystical space where the normal rules don't apply. So you still have a duty of care towards children who might feel vulnerable.

Don't force a child to be the "native informant" for a minority perspective, for example, "So Roxana, Ben's asking why you can wear a headscarf when he can't wear a baseball cap?"

Introduce an exhibit or witness into the enquiry to provide an absent voice, using text, a youtube clip, or another adult.

Have an empty chair - and ask who the class would want to have sitting in it to supply a missing viewpoint. Then you or volunteers take on that role.

Act as the clerk to the enquiry to bring in some needed facts.

The Benefits of P4C

A four year P4C project in Clackmannanshire was evaluated by a team of educational psychologists led by Steven Trickey (Google "Trickey Linkopings"). They used standardised tests and analyses of questionnaires and videos. Confirming earlier research, they found benefits of regular P4C included:

- Cognitive gains – higher scores on CATS tests.

- Improved self-esteem as learners.

- Increasing use of reasons to support answers.

- Pupils doing a greater share of the talking compared to teachers.

- Teachers using more open-ended questions.

- Improved communication skills, confidence and concentration.

- Better self-management of feelings and impulsivity.

- Effects that lasted after P4C had stopped

There are many scholars in the UK and elsewhere working in P4C and several universities offer Masters modules and PhD programs mentored by P4C specialists. Other findings are mentioned on **www.sapere.org.uk** and **www.p4c.com**

The Spirit of Enquiry

Matthew Lipman, the originator of P4C, once sent a note to a conference with just one line, "The Spirit of Enquiry". Facilitating P4C means infusing your practice with that spirit far more than following particular procedures. What might that spirit be?

Enquiry is not debate. In a debate, if you change your mind you have lost the argument. In an enquiry, a change of mind is a sign of growth and engagement.

Enquiry is live and responsive - like telling rather than reading a story, only more so. That makes it bracingly unpredictable. When preset learning objectives are supposed to tie down every minute of the school day, the chance to follow the thinking where it leads is like being released into the wild.

Enquiry is serious. It relishes difficulty and challenge. The puzzles it deals with are to do with wonder and a desire to make sense of things, not idle amusement. At the same time, it is playful and subversive. It allows people to experiment with ideas, contemplate outlandish possibilities and question their own thinking and that of authorities.

Above all, what makes enquiry contagious is that it is a special way of being with others. Whether children or adults, in philosophical enquiry people connect with one another as they really are, rather than as masks sent to negotiate with other masks. It is a space where minds meet working at their best.

www.p4c.com is an excellent subscription website with a bank of resources searchable by key stage and theme. There is some useful stuff in its free guest area too, including some videos of P4C sessions.

www.teachingchildrenphilosophy.org by Tom Wartenberg has some excellent discussion plans for picture books.

Sara Stanley's "But Why?" is a must for teachers of younger children. Robert Fisher's "...for thinking" series is also popular.

If you are interested in exploring the academic tradition of philosophy, try Julian Baggini's "The Pig that Wants to Be Eaten and 99 Other Thought Experiments".

Jostein Gaarder's "Hello? Is Anybody There?" (primary) and Stephen Law's "Philosophy Files" (secondary) are good for developing a love of juicy questions.

Going back to original sources, if you'd like to try some philosophy raw, Hume's "Dialogues Concerning Natural Religion" (Penguin edition) is very readable.

A wider range of teacher resources, introductions to philosophy and picture books chosen for P4C can be viewed and bought from my Amazon Store: www.tinyurl.com/p4cbooks

SAPERE
communities of enquiry

SAPERE is the Society for Advancing Philosophical Enquiry and Reflection in Education. It was founded in 1992 after interest in P4C was roused by the BBC documentary 'Socrates for Six Year Olds', and became a charity in 1993. It is affiliated to the International Association for Philosophy for Children.

It supports the work of practitioners and trainers in philosophy for children and communities by conducting research, coordinating projects, running conferences, convening groups of P4Cers with similar interests, running and accrediting courses, commissioning resources and providing CPD and quality assurance for a network of trainers.

You can support the work of SAPERE and join a growing network of P4Cers and supporters by becoming a member. Members receive:

- Access to an online resource bank
- Annual printed newsletter and monthly e-bulletins
- Preferential rates for SAPERE events
- Networking opportunities and support

For details of membership, visit
www.sapere.org.uk or ring 01865 811184.

the **philosophy** man

P4C hadn't reached Essex in my youth, which is perhaps why I left sixth form to teach myself before reading philosophy at Cambridge. Next, a bizarre series of jobs and enterprises including selling fireworks and not selling encyclopaedias. Eventually I became a philosophy-flavoured English teacher.

Now I am a freelance P4C writer, trainer and pupil workshop host. One ongoing project is giving teachers sustained support to make thinking fun, through a free, most-weekly email bulletin of stories and resources. The enquiry plan and materials for the example on pgs 3-4 are in Issue 1, and examples of other techniques such as the "Evilometer" are in succeeding issues. To receive it, enter your name and email on the homepage of:

www.thephilosophyman.com

You are also welcome to contact me with your P4C queries, requests, suggestions, problems and triumphs on my mobile, 07843 555355 or at jason@thephilosophyman.com

If you would like me to work with your school, please get in touch as early as you can. I juggle bookings with running day and residential courses for gifted children (giftcourses.co.uk) and an outdoor education company (outspark.co.uk). You can see all my projects and enterprises at www.jasonbuckley.co.uk